MODERN SOCIALISM

MODERN SOCIALISM

BY
ANNIE BESANT

GYAN

ISBN: 978-81-212-1896-2 (HB)
First Published, 1886
Published, 2018
Published by

Gyan Publishing House
5, Ansari Road
Daryaganj, New Delhi-110002
Phone: 011-47034999, 9811692060
www.gyanbooks.com
E-mail: books@gyanbooks.com

Printed at: G. Print Process, Delhi.

MODERN SOCIALISM.

GREAT changes are long in the preparing, and every thought that meets ultimately with wide acceptance is lying inarticulate in many minds ere it is syllabled out by some articulate one, and stands forth a spoken Word. The *Zeitgeist* has its mouth in those of its children who have brain to understand, voice to proclaim, courage to stand alone. Some new Truth then peals out, sonorous and far-sounding as the roll of the thunder, melodious to the ears attuned to the deep grand harmonies of Nature, but terrible to those accustomed only to the subdued lispings of artificial triflers, and the murmurs which float amid the hangings of courtly halls.

When such an event occurs a few hearken, study, and then rejoicingly accept the new Truth; these are its pioneers, its apostles, who go out to proclaim it to the as yet unbelieving world. They meet with ridicule, then with persecution; for ever the new Truth undermines some hoary Lie, which has its band of devoted adherents living on the spoils of its reign. Slowly, against custom and tradition, against selfishness and violence, even against indifference, deadliest foe of all, this band of devoted teachers makes its onward way. And the band grows and grows, and each convert becomes in his turn a pioneer; until at last the victory is won, and the minority has become the majority; and then the time comes for some new Truth once more, and the old struggle is gone over afresh, and so again and again; and thus the race makes progress, and humanity climbs ever upward towards the perfect life.

During the last century and a quarter the social problem has been pressing for solution on all who have brains to think and hearts to feel. The coexistence of wealth and penury, of idle prodigality and laborious stint; the terrible fact that "progress and poverty" seem to march hand-in-hand; the growing slums in large towns; the huge fortunes and the starving poor; these things make content impossible, and force into prominence the question: "Must this state of things continue? Is there no possible change which will cure, not only palliate, the present evils?

Great hopes have sprung into being from time to time, each in turn to be blighted. Machinery was to double production and diminish toil, to spread comfort and sufficiency everywhere. It made cotton-lords and merchant-princes with one hand, and with the other created a proletariat unlike aught the world had seen, poor in the midst of the wealth it created, miserable in the midst of luxury, ignorant in the midst of knowledge, savage in the midst of civilisation. When the repeal of the Corn Laws was striven for and accomplished, once more hope rose high. Cheap food was to put an end to starvation. Alas! in the streets of the wealthiest city in Christendom, men and women perish for lack of a loaf of bread.

Nor is this persistence of misery and of squalor the only sign which troubles the brain and the heart of the student of the social problem. He notes the recurring crises in industry, the inflations and depressions of trade. At one time all is prosperous; demand is brisk, and supply can scarce keep pace with it; wages rise, full time is worked, production is enormously increased. Then a change creeps over all; supply has overtaken, has surpassed demand; the market is glutted; the warehouses are filled with unsaleable goods; short time begins; wages fall; mills are closed; furnaces are damped out; many workers are discharged. Then the unemployed in the large towns increase in number; the poor-rate rises; distress spreads upwards. After a while the depression passes; trade improves; and the whole weary circle is trodden once more. Nor is this all; although there has been "over-production" there is want of the necessaries of life; there are unsaleable clothing goods in the warehouses, and half-naked people shivering outside; too many blankets, and children crying themselves to sleep for cold. This monstrous absurdity, of commodities a drug in the market, and human beings perishing for want of those very commodities, stares us ever in the face. Cannot human brain discover some means to put an end to this state of things, a state which would be ludicrous were it not for the horrible suffering involved in it? Some say, this must always be so; that the poor shall be for ever with us; that commercial crises are inevitable; that these evils are not susceptible of complete cure. If this indeed be true, then I know not that any better advice can be given to humanity than that given to Job by his wife, to "curse God and die". But I think not so meanly of human intelligence; I believe not that our present industrial system, little more than a century old, must needs be eternal; I believe that the present system, devised by man and founded in greed of gain, may by man be changed; and that man's growing power over external nature may be used to bring comfort and wealth to each, and not, as now, to enrich the few at the cost of the enslavement of the many.

Various attempts to bring about a better social state have been made by earnest and noble-hearted men during the last hundred years. I leave aside such systems as those of the Moravians, because they cannot be regarded as in any sense schemes for the reconstruction of society. They, like the monastic communities, were merely attempts to create oases, fenced in from the world's evils, where men might prepare for a future life. The efforts I allude to are those classed as "Socialistic"; they were really crude forms of Communism. With these the name of Robert Owen will be for ever associated.

Owen's first experiment was made at New Lanark, in connexion with the cotton-mills established there by Mr. Dale, his father-in-law. He became the manager of these in 1797, and set himself to work to improve the condition of the operatives and their families. The success which attended his efforts, the changes wrought by education and by fair dealings, encouraged him to plan out a wider scheme of social amelioration. In 1817 he was asked to report on the causes of poverty to the Committee on the Poor Laws, and in this report he dwelt on the serious increase of pauperism which had followed the introduction of machinery, and urged that employment ought to be found for those who were in need of it. He "recommended that every union or county should provide a farm for the employment of their poor; when circumstances admitted of it, there should be a manufactory in connexion with it" ("Robert Owen," by A. J. Booth, p. 70). On the farm, buildings were to be built for housing the laborers, consisting of "a square, divided into two parallelograms by the erection of public buildings in the centre"; these would consist of "a kitchen, mess-room, school-rooms, library and lecture-hall. The poor would enjoy every advantage that economy could suggest: the same roof would cover many dwellings: the same stove might warm every room: the food would be cooked at the same time, and on the same fire: the meals would be eaten from the same table, in the society of friends and fellow-workers. Sympathies now restricted to the family would be thus extended to a community: the union would be still further cemented by an equal participation in the profits, an equal share in the toil. . . . . Competition is the cause of many vices; association will be their corrective" (*Ibid*, pp. 70-72). Soon after this report, Mr. Owen published a letter, urging the reconstitution of "the whole of society on a similar basis"; the lowest class was to consist of paupers, to be drafted into the proposed establishments; the second of the "working-class"; the third of laborers, artisans, and tradesmen, with property of from £100 to £2,000; the fourth of persons unable or unwilling to work, owning from £1,000 to £20,000; these were to employ the second class. The workman was to be supported by this class in comfort for seven years in exchange for his labor, and then was to be presented by it with £100, so that he might enter class three; if he remained as a worker for five years more he was to have £200.

A community of workers, as recommended by Owen, was started in 1825, under the management of Abraham Combe, at Orbiston, nine miles east of Glasgow, and it began well; but Combe died in 1827, and with his death the whole thing went to pieces. A few months before the settlement at Orbiston, Robert Owen sailed for America, and he purchased a property named Harmony, consisting of 30,000 acres in Indiana, from the Rappites, a religious communistic body. He advertised for inhabitants, and gathered together a mixed crowd; "there were some enthusiasts who had come, at great personal sacrifice, to face a rude life and to mix among rude men, who had no object but to work out the great problem of a New Society;

there were others who fancied they could secure abundance with little labor, prepared to shirk their share in the toil, but not to forego their share in the reward" (*Ibid*, p. 106). In the following year, 1826, "New Harmony" inaugurated a system of complete Communism, much against Owen's judgment; a number of small independent communities were soon formed, eight of these having already broken off from New Harmony early in 1827, the difficulties attendant on widely extended common life being found insuperable. In 1828, Robert Owen was forced to confess that his efforts had failed, and that "families trained in the individual system" could not suddenly be plunged into pure Communism with success. It boots not to dwell here on his further efforts in England. Robert Owen's experiments failed, but out of his teaching arose the co-operative movement, and the impulse to seek some rational system of society has, since his time, never quite died out in England.

In America a large number of communities have been established, mostly religious in character. From the careful account given of them by Charles Nordhoff, the following brief details are taken (all numbers relate to 1874). The Amana community consists of 1,450 members; they have a property of 25,000 acres, and live in seven small towns; they are Germans, very pious and very prosperous; their head is a woman, who is directly inspired by God. The Harmony Society, Economy, near Pittsburg, consists of followers of Rapp, who founded the society in 1805. They are all Germans and number 110, in addition to about 100 hired laborers and some sixty children. They live in comfort, and have clearly done well unto them-unto themselves, owning now a very large amount of property. The Separatists of Zoar, Ohio, are, once more, Germans: they started in 1817, have now about 300 members, own 7,000 acres of land, and are prosperous exceedingly. The Shakers, established in 1792, are scattered over several States, number about 2,415, own about 100,000 acres of land, are divided into fifty-eight communities, and are wealthy and prosperous; the members are American and English. The Perfectionists of Oneida and Wallingford are American, and the first attempt by them at communal living took place in 1846. They number 521, and own 894 acres of land. They also are prosperous.

The Aurora and Bethel Communes, in Oregon, are German, or "Pennsylvania Dutch"; they started in 1844, and now number some 600 persons: their property extends to 23,000 acres, and they live in much comfort. The Icarians, founded by Etienne Cabet in 1848, are nearly all French; they have hitherto been less fortunate than the preceding societies, in consequence of mismanagement at the start; a heavy debt was incurred early in the movement, and members fell off; but a few resolute men and women settled down steadily in Iowa, with 4,000 acres of land, and 20,000 dollars of debt; they had to give up the land to their creditors, but managed to redeem nearly half of it, and they are now 65 in number, own 1,936 acres, have no debts, and have acquired a large live stock. They still live very plainly, but are on their way to prosperity, having conquered all the difficulties amid which they started; their constitution is perfectly democratic and they are without religion. A Swedish community at Bishop Hill, Illinois, was formed by a pietist sect which emigrated to America to escape persecution in 1846-1848. They were terribly poor at first and lived in holes in the ground, with a tent for a church, but gradually acquired property; until in 1859 they owned 10,000 acres of land, worth 300,000 dollars, and some magnificent live stock. Unfortunately their piety led to such extreme dullness that the younger members of the society revolted: debt was incurred, individuality was advocated, the property was divided, and the community ceased to exist. Lastly, there are two small communities, founded in 1871 and 1874; the former, the Progressive Community, at Cedar Vale, consists partly of Russians; it possesses 320 acres of good land, and has only eight members, of whom one is a child. The second, the Social Freedom Community, consists of three adults and three lads, Americans, and has a farm of 333 acres.

The whole of these societies can only be regarded as in the nature of experiments, and as such they are extremely interesting; each community has succeeded in gaining comfort and independence, but these small bodies, living chiefly by agriculture in a thinly-populated country on virgin soil, while they show the advantages of associated labor, really offer no data for the solution of the problems which beset a complex society. They are a return to more primitive forms of living, not an onward social evolution, and they are only possible in a "new country". Further, while they are communistic so far as their own members are concerned, they are individualistic and competitive in their aspect to the outer world; each small group holds its own property, and transacts all its business on the old lines in its dealings with the rest of the nation. This is, of course, inevitable, since each is encircled by competition; but it must not be overlooked that all these organisations, like co-operative societies at home, are nothing more than enlarged families, and are essentially individualistic; winning sufficiency for their own narrow, isolated circles, but leaving untouched the question of national poverty. They are arks, rescuing their inmates from the deluge, but they do nothing to drain away the seething ocean of misery.

We turn next to Socialism, as distinct from Communism. The distinction between these, though recognised by so orthodox an economist as John Stuart Mill, is generally ignored by those who oppose any radical reconstruction of Society. Mr. Mill divides into two classes the assailants of the present system of purely individualistic property: "those whose scheme implies absolute equality in the distribution of the physical means of life and enjoyment, and those who admit inequality, but grounded on some principle or supposed principle, of justice or general expediency, and not, like so many of the existing social inequalities, dependent on accident alone. At the head of the first class, as the earliest of those belonging to the present generation, must be placed Mr. Owen and his followers. M. Louis Blanc and M. Cabet have more recently become conspicuous as apostles of similar doctrines (though the former advocates equality of distribution only as a transition to a still higher standard of justice, that all should work according to their capacity, and receive according to their wants). The characteristic name for this economical system is Communism, a word of continental origin, only of late introduced into this country. The word Socialism, which originated among the English Communists, and was assumed by them as a name to designate their own doctrine, is now, on the Continent, employed in a larger sense; not necessarily implying Communism, or the entire abolition of private property, but applied to any system which requires that the land and the instruments of production should be the property, not of individuals, but of communities or associations, or of the government" ("Principles of Political Economy", Book II., chap. i., sec. 2). Communism implies the complete abolition of private property, and the supply of the wants of each individual from a common store, without regard to the contributions to that common store which may, or may not, have been made by the individual. Socialism merely implies that the raw material of the soil and the means of production shall not be the private property of individuals, but shall be under the control of the community; it leaves intact a man's control over himself and over the value of his work—subject to such general laws as are necessary in any community—but by socialising land and capital it deprives each of the power of enslaving his fellows, and of living in idleness on the results of their labor instead of on the results of his own. It may be that at some future time humanity shall have evolved to a point which shall render Communism the only rational system; when every man is eager to do his share of work; anxious not to make too much for his own enjoyment; holding the scales of justice with a perfectly even hand; his one aim the general good, and his one effort the service of his brethren; when each individual is thus developed, law will have become unnecessary, and Communism will be the natural expression of social life; perfect freedom will be the lot of each, because each will have become a law unto himself. But to that stage of development man has not yet attained, and for man as he is Communism would mean the living of the idle on the toil of the laborious, the rebirth, under a new name, of our present system.

Modern Socialism is an attempt to get at the root of the poverty which now prevails; to find out how fortunes are made; why commercial crises occur; what are the real relations of capital and labor at the present time.

In speaking of "fortunes", I do not here include fortunes made by gambling, as on the Stock Exchange. They fall under another category, for in gambling, whether on the Stock Exchange or on the card table, wealth is not really made; it only passes from one pocket to another. The gambler, or the burglar, may "make a fortune" so far as he is himself concerned; but it is not done by the creation of wealth, but only by transferring wealth already existing from the pocket of its temporary possessor into his own; in both businesses the profits are large because the risks are great, and the penalty for failure heavy for the moment.

Socialism, as an industrial system, is chiefly concerned with fortunes in the making, with the way in which the wealth created by associated labor passes into the hands of individuals who do little or nothing in exchange for it. These fortunes arise from the ownership of the instruments of production, or of the raw material out of which wealth is to be manufactured; from the ownership, that is, of capital or of land.

Production.

Let us take the case of the possessor of capital employed in manufacture. This man desires to obtain more wealth than he can produce alone, more than he can individually produce even with the help of machinery. He must consequently hire others, who, in exchange for a certain fixed sum to be paid to them by him, shall allow him to take over the whole results of their labor, and to pocket the difference between those results and the fixed sum paid by him. This fixed sum is known as wage, and is "the market price of labor". We have therefore here two classes face to face with each other: one is a class which is the owner of capital, that is, which possesses the instruments of production; the other is a class which possesses the labor-force, without which the instruments of production are useless, but which must perish if it cannot get hold of some of those instruments. (Behind the capitalists is a third class, the land-owning, with which the capitalist has to come to terms; that will be dealt with afterwards.) This second class stands therefore at this disadvantage; that while the capitalist can, if he pleases, utilise his own labor-force for his own subsistence, it cannot subsist at all except with his consent and aid, being shut out from the raw material by the landowner, and from the instruments of production by himself. Put a naked man on fertile soil in a decent climate and he will subsist; he will live on fruit and berries while with his hands he fashions some rough tool, and with the help thereof makes him a better one; out of the raw material he will form an instrument of production with those original instruments of production given him by nature, his fingers and the muscles of his body; then with his instrument and the raw material at his feet he will labor and win his livelihood. But in our complex society this opening is not before him; the raw material is enclosed and trespassers are prosecuted; if he picks fruit for food, he is a thief; if he breaks off a bough to make a rough tool, he is arrested; he cannot get an instrument of production, and if he could he would have nothing to use it on; he has *nothing* but his labor-force, and he must either sell that to someone who wants it, or he must die. And the sale must be complete. His labor-force is bought for so much down per week or per month; it no longer belongs to himself, it is owned by his master, and he has not any right over that which it produces; he has sold it, and if he wants to resume possession he must give notice of his wish to the owner thereof; having resumed possession it is of no use to him; he can only live by selling it to somebody else. He is "free", in so far that he is able to change his master; he is a slave in that he must sell the labor force in his body for food. The man whose labor-force has been sold to another for life is regarded by all as a slave; the man whose labor-force is sold for stated terms is regarded by most as free; yet in comparing the conditions of the two, it is well to bear in mind that the slave, in becoming a chattel, becomes of value to his master, and it is the interest of the latter to feed him well and to keep up his physical strength as long as is possible; also in old age he is fed and housed, and can die in peace amid his fellows. Whereas the wage-earner has no such value, but it is his master's interest to get as much work out of him as is possible, without regard for his health, there being plenty to take his place when he is worn out; and when he is old, he is separated from wife and child and is left to die in the prison we call a workhouse. The slave is valuable, as the horse and the ox are valuable, to his owner; the wage-earner is valuable only as a garment, which is cast into the dusthole when it is worn out.

It may be answered that the wage-earner by good fortune, industry, and thrift, may be able so to save of his earnings that he may escape the workhouse, and may even himself become independent and an "employer of labor". True. So might a lucky slave become free. But the truth that some may rise out of their class does not render satisfactory the state of the class, and the very fact that such rising is held out as a reward and a stimulus is an admission that an escape from the proletariat must be the natural longing of every proletarian. The rising of a few does not benefit the proletariat as a whole, and it is the existence of this unpropertied proletariat which is the evil thing.

To this proletariat, waiting to sell its labor-force, the capitalist goes, for it is here that he will be able to obtain the wealth-making strength which he requires. The next question is: What determines the wage which he is to pay? That is: what fixes the market price of labor-force? Putting on one side temporary and comparatively trivial causes, which may slightly affect it one way or the other, there are two constant determinants: population, and standard of living. The market-price of labor-force will largely depend on the quantity of labor-force in the market; if the supply exceed the demand, the price will be low; if the demand exceed the supply, the price will go up. If an employer requires fifty laborers, and two hundred laborers compete with each other for the employment he offers, and if the employment stands between them and starvation, he will be able to beat down their price until it touches the lowest point at which they can subsist. The more rapid the multiplication of the proletariat, the better for the capitalist class.

The other determinant is the "standard of living" or "standard of comfort". Wage can never sink beyond the point at which a man and his family can exist thereon; this is the extreme limit of its fall, inasmuch as a man will not work unless he can exist on the results of his work. As a matter of fact, it does not often sink so low; the wage of an ordinary operative is more than barely suffices to keep him and his family alive, but large numbers of the laboring poor are habitually underfed, and are liable to the diseases brought on by low living, as well as to premature aging and death arising from the same cause. It is a significant fact that the deathrate of the poor is much higher than the deathrate of the rich. Wage is lower in countries in which the standard of living is low, than in those in which it is, by comparison, higher. Thus in parts of Scotland, where oatmeal is much used for food, and children run much barefoot, wage is normally lower than in England, where wheaten flour and shoes and stockings are expected. Any general lowering of the standard of living is therefore to be deprecated—as the wide substitution of cheap vegetable food-stuffs for more expensive articles of diet. The standard of living also (and chiefly, in any given country) affects wages through its effect on population. Mill points out ("Principles of Political Economy," Book II., chap. xi., sec. 2) that "wages do adapt themselves to the price of food", either (*a*) from children dying prematurely when food rises, and wages were before barely sufficient to maintain them, or (*b*) from voluntary restriction of the growth of population when the laborers refuse to sink below a certain standard of living. In each case the diminution of labor supply causes a rise of wage. "Mr. Ricardo", says Mill, "considers these two cases to comprehend all cases. He assumes, that there is everywhere a minimum rate of wages: either the lowest with which it is physically possible to keep up the population, or the lowest with which the people will choose to do so. To this minimum he assumes that the general rate of wages always tends; that they can never be lower, beyond the length of time required for a diminished rate of increase to make itself felt, and can never long continue higher." This is the "iron law of wages", and it is the recognition of its truth which, among other reasons, sets Socialists against the wage-system of industry. [It must not be forgotten that the phrase "ordinary operative" does not include all the workers. There is a large class which obtains barely subsistence wage, and those who are not regularly employed are on the very verge of starvation. The hard lot of these must not be left out of sight in impeaching the present social state.]

The capitalist, then, buys as much labor-force as he desires, or as his means allow, at the market price, determined in the way we have seen. This labor-force he proposes to utilise for his own advantage; with some of his capital he buys it; some of his capital consists in machinery, and the labor-force set at work on this machinery is to produce wealth. The labor-force and the instruments of production are now brought together; they will now produce wealth, and both they and the wealth they produce are the property of the capitalist.

Our next inquiry is: Where does the capitalist look for his profit? He has bought machinery; he has bought labor-force; whence comes the gain he is seeking? The profit of the capitalist must arise from the difference between the price he pays for labor-force and the wealth produced by it; out of this difference must be paid his rent, the loss incurred by wear-and-tear, and the price of the raw material on which his machinery works; these provided for, the remainder of the difference is his "profit". The analysis of the way in which this profit arises is, then, the task that comes next.

In Karl Marx's "Das Capital" may be found a carefully elaborated exposition of "surplus-value". The term is a convenient one, and the student will do well to read his 7th chapter, on the "production of use-value and surplus-value"; in reading, he must remember Marx's definitions of value and use-value, which of course govern the whole. Value is human labor incorporated in a commodity; use-value is that which in a commodity satisfies some human want. The "use-value" of Marx is identical with the "intrinsic natural worth" of Locke. Locke says: "The intrinsic, natural worth of any thing, consists in its fitness to supply the necessities, or serve the conveniences of human life" ("Considerations of the Lowering of Interest," etc., Locke's Works, vol. ii., p. 28, ed. 1777). As an instance of the production of surplus-value—that is of the difference between the capital which the capitalist expends in production and that which he possesses when the production is complete—Marx takes the case of the manufacture of ten pounds of thread. The capitalist buys ten pounds of cotton at 10s.; wear-and-tear of machinery in the spinning of the cotton into thread raises his expenditure to 12s.; further, six hours of work are necessary to turn the ten pounds of cotton into ten pounds of thread.

Now suppose that a man in six hours is able to produce sufficient to maintain himself for a day;—that is that he produces as much as might be exchanged for a day's consumption of the necessaries of life. Let us value this at 3s. in money. That 3s. which is the monetary equivalent of his six hours' labor must be added to the cost of production of the thread; its value has therefore risen finally to 15s. If the capitalist now sells his ten pounds of thread for 15s., he will only receive back as much as he has expended; he will have made no profit. But suppose the working day be of twelve hours instead of six, the wages paid will none the less be fixed at 3s. by the standard of living; but in that second six hours the operative can transform another ten pounds of cotton into another ten pounds of thread; as before, cotton and wear-and-tear will amount to 12s.; but these ten pounds of thread have a value of 15s. as had the previous ten pounds, although they have only cost the capitalist 12s. Hence the final product of the day's labor has a value of 30s., but has cost the capitalist only 27s. The value added by the operative in the second six hours has brought *him* no equivalent; it is "surplus-value", value added by him over the value whose equivalent he receives in wage; this creation of surplus-value is the aim of the capitalist.

Now without tying ourselves down to the exact figures given by Marx, we may yet see by a little thought that his position as to "surplus-value" is essentially correct. If a capitalist buys £1 worth of raw material; if his machinery is depreciated say by the value of one shilling in working up the raw material; if he pays in wage 5s. for the labor-force expended on it; he will most certainly not be content with selling the finished product for 26s. He demands a "profit" on the transaction, and this profit can only be the difference between that which is paid to labor, and the value, in the ordinary sense of the word, which labor creates.

It is sometimes objected that nothing is gained by Marx's divisions of "value", "surplus value", and "exchange value", but that, on the contrary, they transport economics into a metaphysical region away from the solid ground of facts. It is urged that it is better to represent the conditions thus: that the worker produces a mass of commodities; that the capitalist sells these commodities for what they will fetch in the market, the price being fixed, not by the duration of the labor embodied in them, but by the relative utilities of money and commodity to buyer and seller; that the capitalist gives over to the producer sufficient of the results of the sale to enable the producer to exist, and pockets the remainder. This presentment is a statement of the facts as they are; Marx's "value" is a metaphysical abstraction, corresponding to nothing existing at the present time, however true it would be under ideal conditions. The main point to grasp, however, is obvious, whichever of these presentments is thought preferable. Capital, under our present industrial system, is the result of unpaid labor—a matter to be further considered later in this essay. But it must be remembered that, as a matter of fact, the profit made by the capitalist is not a fixed quantity, as is the "surplus value" of Marx; but that the capitalist not only preys on the worker, but also on the necessities of the consumer, his profit rising and falling with the changes of demand and supply. The phrase "surplus value" is, as I have said, a convenient one, but it might well be extended to cover the whole difference between the price paid to labor for the commodities it produces, and the price obtained for those commodities by the capitalist employer of labor. It is in this wide sense that the phrase is used in the following pages, not in the metaphysical sense of Marx.

We are now in a position to understand how large fortunes are made, and why Capital and Labor are ever at war.

Before the commencement of the Industrial Period—which may be fairly dated from the invention of the Spinning Jenny in 1764—it was not possible to accumulate great wealth by the employment of hired labor. By hand-work, or by the use of the very simple machines available prior to that date, a single operative was not able to produce sufficient to at once support himself and to largely enrich others. "Masters and men" consequently formed a community of workers, without the sharp divisions that now exist between capitalist and "hands"; and the employer would have been as much ashamed of *not* working deftly at his trade, as the son of a Lancashire cotton-lord would be if he were suspected of throwing a shuttle in one of his father's looms. Under these conditions there was very little surplus-value to be absorbed, and there were consequently no great aggregations of purely industrial classes. The introduction of machinery multiplied enormously the productive power of the operative, while it did not increase the wage he received. A man receiving 3s. for a day of twelve hours, produced, we will say for the sake of illustration, surplus-value to the amount of 1s.; after the introduction of machinery he received the same wage and produced an enormously increased surplus-value.

Thus the fortunes of the lucky possessors of the new machinery rose by "leaps and bounds"; lads who began at the loom were owners of palaces by middle age; even later on, after the first rush had spent itself, I have myself met Lancashire cotton-lords who were mill-hands in their youth; but most certainly their wealth had only been made by the results of the toil of many becoming concentrated in the hands of one.

Another step was taken to increase surplus-value. Depending, as it does, on the difference between the value produced by the worker and the amount paid to him as wage, it is obvious that if it be possible to obtain the same amount of produce from purchased labor-force while reducing the purchase-money, the surplus-value will become larger. This step was soon taken, for it was found that many machines could be superintended by a woman quite as effectively as by a man, while female labor-force was purchasable in the market at a lower rate. Hence the large introduction of female "hands" into cotton mills, and as married women were found more "docile" than unmarried—docility increasing with the number of mouths crying for bread at home—there came the double curse on the producers, of male labor being pushed aside by female labor at lower wage, and of untidy home and neglected children, bereft of mother's care. Yet another step. Child-labor was cheaper even than woman-labor, and by utilising children, with their pitiful wage, surplus-value might be swollen to yet larger proportions; and as wives had fought with husbands for wage, so children now fought with fathers and mothers, until verily a man's foes in the labor-market were they of his own household.

There was, however, a way of increasing surplus-value apart from the amount of daily wage. The lengthening of the hours of labor has obviously the same result in this respect as the lowering of wage. The very zenith of the production of surplus-value, the most complete exploitation of the producers, the perfect triumph of the capitalist ideal of free contract and of *laissez-faire*, were reached when little children, at nominal wage, were worked from fifteen to sixteen hours a day, and princely fortunes were built up by human sacrifice to the devil of greed, in fashion that shall never, so help us tongue, and pen, and arm, be again possible in this fair English land.

We have at the present time no exact figures available which can enable us to judge of the precise amount of surplus value produced in the various departments of industry. In America, the Bureaus of Labor Statistics help us, and from these we learn some suggestive facts.

	Average wage paid to worker.	Extra net value produced by worker.
1850	£49 12	£41 16
1860	58 8	65 10
1870	62 0	69 0
1880	69 4	64 14

(Taken from Laurence Gronlund's quotation of these returns in his "Co-operative Commonwealth", chap. i. The same figures, as regards total net produce and wages paid, have appeared in a capitalist work.) I trust that we shall soon have in England Labor Bureaus similar to those now existing in the United States and in Canada. Charles Bradlaugh, M.P., has succeeded in passing a resolution in favor of the official publication of similar statistics through the House of Commons, and among the many priceless services he has done to the workers, the obtaining of these is by no means the least. Exact knowledge of the present state of things is a necessary precedent of organic change, and the figures supplied by the Labor Bureaus will give us the very weapons that we need.

The absolutely antithetical interests of Capital and Labor have necessitated—and must continue to necessitate while the present system lasts—a constant and embittered war. As Capital can only grow by surplus value, it strives to lengthen the working day and to decrease the daily wage. Labor struggles to shorten the hours of toil, and to wring from Capital a larger share of its own product in the form of higher wage. While Capital is the possession of one class, and Labor is the only property of the other, this strife must go on. There can never be industrial peace until this root of war be pulled up, and until Capital, under the control of the community, shall be used for the fertilisation, instead of for the oppression of Labor.

Since large fortunes are made by manufacturers, and there is no source of wealth save labor applied to natural objects, it is clear that these fortunes are due to the fact that the manufacturers are able to become the owners of the means of production and of labor-force; even these very means of production, with which the present labor-force works, are but past labor-force crystallised. The wage-earners must produce sufficient to maintain themselves from day to day and to increase the capital of the wage-payers, else they will not be employed. Hence arises another evil, the waste of productive force. Men are not employed because their labor-force, embodied in the necessaries of life, will spread sufficiency and comfort throughout the community. They are only employed when the articles produced can be *sold at a profit* by a third party; their products, fairly exchanged for the products of their fellow-laborers—woven cloth, say, for shoes—would clothe warmly the shivering population; but above the cloth produced by the one, and the shoes produced by the other, stand the capitalists, who demand profit for themselves ere the cloth shall be allowed to shield the naked back, or the shoes keep off the pavement the toes blued by the frost. If the employment fails, the wage-earner is out of food; but the erstwhile wage-payer has the capital made by the former to live upon, while its maker starves. The capitalist, truly, cannot increase his capital, unless he can buy labor-force; but he can live on his capital. On the other hand the labor-force must perish unless it can find a purchaser. Let us put the position plainly, for as the great majority of people think the arrangement a perfectly fair one, there is no need to cover it over with a veil of fine phrases and roundabout expressions. The owner of raw material and of the means of production faces the unpropertied proletarian, and says to him: "I hold in my hands the means of existence; unless you can obtain the means of existence you will die; but I will only let you have them on one condition. And that is that you shall labor for me as well as for yourself. For each hour that you spend in winning bread, you shall spend another in enriching me. I will give you the right to win a hard existence by your labor, if you will give me the right to take whatever you produce beyond that bare existence. You are perfectly free to choose; you can either accept my terms, and let me live on your work, or you can refuse my terms, and starve." Put so baldly, the proposition has a certain brutality in it. Yet when we Socialists argue that a system is bad which concentrates the means of existence in the hands of a propertied class, and leaves an unpropertied class under the hard condition of winning only the right to exist on such terms as may be granted by the propertied; when we urge this, we are told that we are incendiaries, thieves, idiots, or, at the mildest, that our hopes of freeing these enslaved ones are dreams, mere castles in the air.

We have now reached the foundation of modern Socialism. We say: As long as the industrial classes are divided into capitalists and proletarians, so long must continue the present strife, and the present extremes of wealth and of poverty. It is not a mere modification, but a complete revolution of the industrial system which is required. Capital must be controlled by labor, instead of controlling it. The producers must obtain possession of their own product, and must regulate their own labor. The present system has been weighed in the balances and found wanting, and on the wall of the capitalist banqueting-room is written by the finger of modern thought, dipped in the tears and in the bloody sweat of the over-tasked proletariat: "Man hath numbered thy kingdom and finished it. It is divided among the myriads thou hast wronged."

COMPETITION.

Strife is the normal condition of the whole industrial world; Capital strives against Labor, and Labor against Capital, lock-outs and strikes being the pitched battles of the struggle; capitalists strive against capitalists for profits, and the list of the vanquished may be read in the bankruptcy court; workers strive against workers for wage, and injure their own order in the fratricidal combat. Everywhere the same struggle, causing distress, waste, hatred, in every direction; brothers wronging brothers for a trifling gain; the strong trampling down the weak in the frantic race for wealth. It is the struggle of the wild beasts of the forest transferred to the city; the horrible struggle for existence, only in its "civilised" form hearts are wrenched and torn instead of limbs.

It is constantly urged that competition is advantageous because it develops capacity, and by the struggle it causes it brings about the survival of the fittest. The allegation may be traversed on two grounds: granting that capacity is developed by struggle, it is yet developed at great cost of suffering, and it would be more worthy of reasoning beings to seek to bring about the capacity and to avoid the suffering; to borrow an illustration which suggests itself by the very word "struggle", we know that actual fighting develops muscle, endurance, readiness of resource, quickness of the senses; none the less do we regard war as a disgrace to a civilised people, and we find that the useful capacities developed by it may be equally well developed in the gymnasium and the playing-field, without the evils accompanying war. So may education take the place of competition in developing useful qualities. Further we deny that "the fittest" for social progress survive in the competitive struggle. The hardest, the keenest, the most unscrupulous, survive, because such are the fittest for the brutal strife; but the generous, the magnanimous, the just, the tender, the thoughtful, the sympathetic, the very types in whose survival lies the hope of the race, are crushed out. In fact, competition *is* war, and the very reasons which move us to endeavor to substitute arbitration for war, should move us to endeavor to substitute co-operation for competition.

But it is urged, competition among capitalists is advantageous to the public, and it is shown that where two or three railway lines compete for custom, the public is better served than where there is only one. Granted. There is an old adage which says that "when thieves fall out, honest men come by their own"; none the less is it better to stop thieving, than to encourage it under the hope that the thieves may fall out, and some of the stolen goods be recovered. So long as capitalists are permitted to exploit labor, so long is it well that they should compete with each other and so have their profits lessened; but it would be still better to stop the exploitation. Accepting the railway instance, it may be rejoined that the German State railways have comfortable carriages that can hold their own against all comers, and that whereas a railway company, eager for dividends, can only be forced into providing decent carriages by fear of losing customers to a rival, a State railway is managed for the benefit of the public, and improvements are readily introduced. Our post-office system shows how improvements are made without any pressure of competition; it has given us cheaper postage, cheaper telegraphing, and is giving us cheaper parcel-delivery; so that we can send from London a letter to Wick for a penny, a telegram thither for sixpence, and a parcel for threepence; it is a matter of pride to the Postmaster-General of the day, as a public servant, to improve his department, although he is protected by law (save in the case of parcels, only just undertaken) from competition.

Even some economists who approve of competition see the need of limiting its excesses. Mr. R. S. Moffat, for instance, approves of it and thinks that "competition is not only the best, but the only practical means of meeting" "the conflicting natural conditions, between the exigencies of an unknown demand and the fluctuations of an uncertain supply", "that ever has been, or is ever likely to be, discovered" ("The Economy of Consumption," p. 114, ed. 1878). Yet Mr. Moffat points out that "the material cost of competition includes two items: first, superfluous production, or wasted labor; and secondly, ill-balanced distribution, or misdirected labor" (p. 115); and he declares: "Not content with promoting a healthful industry, it enforces tyrannous laws upon labor, and exacts from the free laborer an amount of toil which the hardest taskmaster never succeeded in wringing from the slave. It disturbs by its excesses the balance of industry which its moderation had established. In times of prosperous production it accumulates stocks till they become a nuisance and a source of the most serious embarrassment to producers, who do not know where to turn for employment to their productive resources; and in adverse times it gambles with them, and deprives consumption of their support at the very time for which they were provided" (pp. 116, 117). "It is upon laborers", he says, "not only as individuals, but as a class, that the great burden of over-production falls" (p. 119).

I propose to consider, I., the evils of competition; II., the remedy proposed by Socialism.

I.—The Evils.—Many of these lie on the surface; others become palpable on very slight investigation. They affect the capitalist manufacturer; the distributor; the consumer; and the producing classes.

An ingenious capitalist sees a want and devises an article to meet it; or he devises an article and sets to work to create the want. He places his article before the public, and a demand for it arises. The article either supplies a real want, or it becomes "the fashion", and the demand increases and outstrips the supply. Other capitalists rush in to compete for the profit which is to be made; capital flows rapidly into the particular industry concerned; high wages are offered; operatives flock to it; the supply swells until it overtops the demand. But when this point is touched, the supply is not at once lessened; so long as there is any hope of profit, the capitalists manufacture; wage is lessened to keep up the profit, but this expedient fails; short hours are worked; at last the market becomes thoroughly overstocked. Then distress follows, and while capital seeks new outlets, the operatives fall into the great army of unemployed; and very often the small capitalists, who went into the rush just when profit was at its highest, and who have not sufficient capital to hold out against the fall, and to await a rise, meet the fate of earthenware pots, carried down a torrent among iron ones. When this happens, the result of their speculative folly is held up as an example of the "risks run by capitalists". Nor is this the only way along which a small capitalist sometimes travels to the bankruptcy court. He often borrows money "to extend his business", and if the business shrinks instead of expanding, he becomes bankrupt. In the universal war, the big capitalist fish devour the small fry.

And, after all, even the "successful man" of our competitive society is not one whose lot is to be envied by the healthy human being. Not for him the pure joy in natural beauty, in simple amusements, in intellectual triumph, which is the dower of those unstained by the fight for gold. For the successful competitor in commercial war Nature has no laurel-crown. He has bartered himself for a mess of pottage, and his birthright of healthy humanity is gone from him for evermore. Well does Moffat write his fate: "The man who strives to make a fortune contemplates his own ease and enjoyment, not the good of society. He flatters himself that through his superior skill, tact, wisdom, energy, or whatever quality it is he thinks himself twice as strong in as his neighbors, he will be able to do in half a lifetime what it takes them their whole lives to do. For this he toils and sacrifices his health; for this he rushes upon reckless speculations, and hazards his character and reputation; for this he makes himself indifferent to the rights and callous to the feelings of others; for this he is sordid, mean, and parsimonious.

All these are the means by which, according to different temperaments, the same end is pursued. And what is the end? An illusion, nay, worse, a dishonesty. The man who pursues a fortune is not qualifying himself for any other course of life besides that which he at present lives. He is merely striving to escape from duty into enjoyment. And the fever of the strife frequently becomes his whole existence; so that when he has obtained his object, he finds himself unable to do without the excitement of the struggle" (p. 220). Surely in judging the merits of a system it is fair to take into account the injuries it works to its most successful products. Its masterpieces are the withered and dehumanised; its victims are the paupers and the suicides.

Nor can we leave out of account in studying competitive production the waste of material, and of the time spent in working it up, which result from over-production. The accumulation of stock while the demand is lessening means the making and storing of unneeded wares. Some of these are forced into the market, some lie idly in the great warehouses. The retail dealers find themselves over-stocked, their shelves laden with unsaleable goods. These fade, and spoil, and rust away—so much good material wasted, so much human labor spent for nought, monuments of a senseless system, of the barbarous, uncalculating blindness of our productive force.

More heavily yet than on the capitalist does competition press on the distributor. A dozen traders compete for the custom which one could satisfactorily supply. The competition for shops in a thickly populated neighborhood drives up the rent, and so adds to the retailer's burden. He is compelled to spend large sums in advertising, striving by brilliancy of color or eccentricity of design to impress himself on the public mind. An army of commercial travellers sweeps over the country, each man with his hand against his neighbor in the same trade, pushing, haggling, puffing his own, depreciating his rival's wares. These agents push their goods on the retailer, often when no real demand for them is coming from the public, and then the retailer puffs them, to create a demand on his supply. Nor must we omit from notice the enormous waste of productive energy in this army of canvassers, advertisers, bill-posters, multiplied middlemen of every kind. The distributive work done by these is absurdly out of proportion to their number. We see several carriers' carts half-filled, instead of half the number filled; each carrier has to deliver goods over the whole of a wide area, so that a man may have to drive five miles to deliver a single parcel at a house a stone's throw from a rival office. Yet each man must receive his full day's wage, and must be paid for the hours he is compelled to waste, as well as for those he spends in useful work. It is the same thing in every business. Three or four carts of each trade daily down each road, covering the same ground, supplying each one house here and one there, losing time, wearing out horses and traps, a foolish shameful waste. And all these unnecessary distributors are consumers when they might be producers, and are actually making unnecessary work for others as well as for themselves.

Short-sighted people ask: Would you add all these to the crowds of half-starving unemployed now competing for work? No, we answer. We would not add them to the *un*employed; it is only in a system of complete competitive anarchy that there could be unemployed labor on the one hand, and people clamoring for the necessaries of life on the other. We have already seen that under the present system men are only employed where some profit can be made out of them by the person who hires them. Under a saner system there would be none unemployed while the food and clothing supply was insufficient, and the turning of non-productive consumers into productive ones would only mean shorter hours of labor, since the labor necessary to supply the consumption of the population would be divided among a larger number than before. If wealth be the result of labor applied to raw material, poverty may come from the pressure of population on the raw material which limits the means of subsistence, but never from the greater part of the population working to produce wealth on raw material sufficient for their support.

On the consumer falls much of the needless additional expense of advertisements, canvassers, and the rest. The flaming advertisements we see on the walls we pay for in the price of the puffed articles we buy. The trader feels their burden, and tries to recoup himself by adding a fraction of it to the price of the goods he sells. If he is forced to lower his nominal prices in consequence of the pressure of competition with his rivals, yet by adulteration he can really raise, while he seems to lower, them. The nominal width of fabrics does not correspond with the real; woollen goods are sold of which the warp is cotton; tobacco is sold damped unfairly to increase its weight; sand is mixed with sugar; lard or dripping with butter; chicory with coffee; sloe-leaves with tea; turnip with orange in marmalade; foreign meat is offered as home-grown; damaged flesh is chopped up for sausages; until, at last, as Moffat caustically remarks: "It is not rogues and vagabonds alone who have recourse in trade to expedients which could not be justified by a strict theoretical morality. When this incline is entered upon, there is no resting upon it. Morality itself becomes subject to competition; and the conventional standard of trade morality gets lower and lower, until the things done by respectable people can hardly be distinguished from those done by people who are not respectable, except by the respectability of the people who do them" (p. 154). And in all this adulteration the consumer suffers in health, comfort, and temper. Not only does he pay more than he should for what he buys, but he buys a good deal more than he pays for.

Heaviest of all is the burden on the operative classes, and they suffer in a double character, both as consumers and producers. As consumers, they share the general injury; as producers, their case is yet more serious. If they are in work, their wages are driven down by the competition for employment; they are the first to feel a lessening demand in lengthened hours, in lower wage; as the depression goes on, they are thrown out of work; illness not only incapacitates them for the time, but their place is filled up, while they lie helpless, by the eager waiters for hire; when they combine to strike for fairer treatment, the fringe of unemployed labor around is used against them by the employers; the lowest depth is reached by the crowd who at the dockyard gates at the East of London literally fight for a place in which the foreman's eye may fall on them, and out of the struggling hundreds units are taken on for the day at miserable wage for heavy exhausting work, to be turned out at night to undergo a similar struggle next morning.

The only classes who gain by competition are the big

capitalists and the landlords. The big capitalists engaged in manufacture gain by the crushing out of their smaller rivals, and by their ability to hold over stocks produced when wages are low until prices are high. Capitalists who only lend out money on usury, and live on the interest thereby obtained, flourish when the demand for money is brisk. Most of all do landlords, who live on rent, profit by the struggle. In a growing neighborhood rents of commercial premises rise rapidly, and the shopkeeper finds himself heavily taxed by the landlord, who imposes on him practically a graduated income-tax for his own advantage. Thus the chief gainers by competition are the idlers who are permitted to hold the nation's soil, and who live in luxury on the toilers, laughing to see how the fratricidal struggles of those who labor turn to the advantage of those who lounge. And so the strain of living constantly increases for the one class, while the luxury and ostentation of those who levy tax on toil become ever greater, and more aggressive by the contrast.

II. The Remedy.—These evils can be radically cured only in one way; it is by the substitution of co-operation for competition, of organisation for anarchy in industry. The relation of employer and employed must disappear, and a brotherhood of workers, associated for facilitation of production for use, must replace the band of servants toiling for the enrichment of a master by profit. The full details of socialised industry cannot be drawn at length; but it is not difficult to see that the already existent co-operative societies offer a suggestive model, and the trades unions a sufficiently competent means for change. Probably each industry in each district will organise itself, and own, for use, all its means of production; thus the miners of Durham, for instance, organised in their lodges, with their central executive, would form the mining trade society of that district; all the mines of that district would be under their control, and they would elect their officers of all grades. So with all mining districts throughout the land. These separate trade societies would be federated, and a General Board elected by all. The elements of such a self-organised industry exist at the present time, and the more closely the miners can band themselves into district unions, and the unions into a national federation, the more prepared will they be to play their part in the great industrial revolution. It is probable that something of the nature of the royalties now paid to the individual mine-owners will be paid into the National Exchequer, in exchange for the right to work the national soil. A similar organisation would be needed for each productive industry, and probably representatives of each separate industry would form a central Industrial Board. But, I repeat, these details cannot now be laid down authoritatively, any more than the details of the present industrial competitive system could have been laid down before the Industrial Period. On these details Socialists would inevitably differ considerably at the present time, and no special scheme can be fairly stamped as "Socialist" to the exclusion of the rest. But on this main principle all Socialists are agreed; that the only rightful holders of capital are industrial groups, or one great industrial group —the State, *i.e.*, the organised community; that while individuals may hold private property for use, none should hold capital—that is *wealth employed in production*—for individual profit; that while each may have property to consume and to enjoy, none should be allowed to use property to enslave his neighbor, to force another to work for his advantage.

The revolution in distribution will be as great as that in production, and here again co-operation must take the place of competition. We already see the beginnings of a distributive change in the establishment of huge stores for the supply of all the necessaries of life, and the way in which these are crushing out the smaller retail shops. Housewives find it more convenient to go to the single building, than to trudge wearily from shop to shop. Goods bought in very large quantities can be sold more cheaply than if bought in small, and economy, as well as convenience, attract the purchaser to the store. At present these stores are founded by capitalists and compete for custom, but they are forerunners of a rational distributive system. The very enmity they create in the minds of the small traders they ruin is paving the way for the community to take them over for the general advantage. Under Socialism all goods manufactured by the producers would be distributed to the central store of each district; from this central store they would be distributed to the retail stores. Anyone who thinks such distribution impossible had better study the postal system now existing; we do not have post-offices jostling each other as do baker's and butcher's shops: there are sufficient of them for the requirements of the district, and no more. The letters for a town are delivered at the General Post Office; they are sorted out and delivered at the subordinate offices; the distribution of the correspondence of millions is carried on by a Government Department, quietly, effectively, without waste of labor, with celerity and economy. But then in the Post Office co-operation has replaced competition, organisation has replaced anarchy. Such a system, one hundred years ago, would have been pronounced impossible, as the Conservative minds of to-day pronounce impossible its extension to anything except letters and telegrams and parcels. I look for the time when the success of the Post Office will be repeated—and improved—in every department of distribution.

Capital.

We have already seen that Capital is accumulated by withholding from the producer a large part of the value he produces, and we have now to look more closely into the growth of Capital and the uses to which it is put. A glance over the historical Past, as well as the study of the Present, inform us that Capital has always been—as indeed it always must be—obtained from unpaid labor, or, if the phrase be preferred, by the partial confiscation of the results of labor. In communities the economic basis of which was slave-labor, this fact was obvious; the owner confiscated the whole products of his slaves' toil, and he became a capitalist by this process of continued confiscation; while the slave, fed, clothed, and housed out of the fruit of his own labor by his master, never owned anything as of right, nor had any property in that which he created. As civilisation advanced, serf-labor replaced slave-labor; here also the confiscation of the results of labor was obvious. The serf was bound to give so many days of work to his lord without payment; this service rendered, the remainder of his time was his own, to produce for his own subsistence; but the lord's capital increased by the confiscation of the results of the serf's labor during the days whereon he worked for his lord. In modern times "free labor" has replaced serf-labor, but in the present industrial system, as truly as in slave and in serf communities, Capital results from unpaid labor, though now from the unpaid labor of the wage-earner. We may search the whole world over, and we shall find no source of wealth save labor applied to natural agents. Wealth is never rained down from heaven, nor is it ever a spontaneous growth; unless indeed wild fruits taken for food be counted wealth, and even to these must human labor be applied in the form of picking ere they can be used. It is the result of human labor; and if one man has more than he has produced, it necessarily follows that another man has less than he has produced. The gain of one must be the loss of another. There are but sixteen court cards in the fifty-two, and if by ingenious shuffling, packing, and dealing, all the court cards fall to one player, only the lower cards can remain for the others.

Separating "Capital" from "Wealth" we may conveniently define it as "wealth devoted to purposes of profit", and as "wealth is the result of labor applied to raw material", Capital becomes the result of labor devoted to purposes of profit. John Stuart Mill says the "accumulated stock of the produce of labor is termed Capital". Macleod: "Capital is any Economic Quantity used for the purpose of Profit". Senior: "Economists are agreed that *whatever* gives a profit is properly called Capital". Something more, however, than the activity of labor is implied in the existence of Capital. There must have been saving, as well as production. Hence Marshall speaks of Capital as "the result of labor and abstinence"; Mill of Capital as "the result of saving"; and so on. It is obvious that if the products of labor were consumed as fast as they were made, Capital could not exist. We have, therefore, reached this certainty when we contemplate Capital; someone has worked, and has not consumed all that he has produced.

Under these circumstances, we should expect to find Capital in the hands of industrious and abstinent producers. But as Mill very justly points out: "In a rude and violent state of society it continually happens that the person who has Capital is not the very person who has saved it, but some one who, being stronger, or belonging to a more powerful community, has possessed himself of it by plunder. And even in a state of things in which property was protected, the increase of Capital has usually been, for a long time, mainly derived from privations which, though essentially the same with saving, are not generally called by that name, because not voluntary. The actual producers have been slaves, compelled to produce as much as force could extort from them, and to consume as little as the self-interest or the usually very slender humanity of their task-masters would permit." How many of our great capitalists have produced and saved until they accumulated the fortunes they possess? These fortunes are greater than any human being could save out of his makings, even if he lived most abstemiously, instead of with the luxury and ostentation of a Rothschild or a Vanderbilt. But if they have not made and saved, how come they to possess? Mill gives the answer, though he did not mean it to be applied to modern industrialism. "In a rude and violent state of society" Capital is not in the hands of the producer and saver, but in the hands of those who possess themselves "of it by plunder"—legalised plunder, in our modern days. The "saving" is not voluntary; it is "derived from privations"; the "actual producers" are wage-earners, who are "compelled to produce as much as" pressure can extort from them, and to "consume as little" in the form of wage as they can be beaten down to by the competition of the labor-market. These men "have labored, and" others "have entered into their labors".

A very brief comparison of those who produce and save, and those who possess themselves of the results of labor and abstinence, will suffice to show the inequality which characterises the present system. The worker lives hardly and dies poor, bequeathing to his children the same necessity of toil: I do not forget that the more fortunate workers have shares in Building Societies, a few pounds in the Savings Bank, and even an interest in a Burial Club, so that the parish may not have the expense of burying them; but I say that these poor successes—vast indeed in the aggregate, but paltry when the share of the individual is looked at—bear no kind of reasonable proportion to the wealth created by the worker during his life-time. On the other hand the capitalist either starts with inherited wealth, grows richer, and bequeaths the increased wealth to his children; or he begins poor, saves a little, then makes others work for him, grows rich, and bequeaths his wealth. In the second generation, the capitalist can simply invest his wealth and live on the interest; and since all interest must be paid out of the results of labor, the workers not only lose a large proportion of their produce, but this very confiscated produce is made into a future burden for them, and while the fathers build up the capitalist, the children must toil to maintain his children in idleness.

Capital may also be accumulated by the ownership of raw material, since no wealth can be produced until labor can get at this. The question of rent will be considered under the head of Land; here we are only concerned with the fact that wealth appropriated in this way is investible, and on this also interest can be obtained.

Now the enormous burden placed on labor by the investment of money at interest, is not appreciated as it ought to be. The interest on the National Debt, including terminable annuities, amounted in 1884–5 to £28,883,672 12s.; how much is paid in dividends on railway, tram-car, and companies' shares, it would be difficult to discover. Mr. Giffen, in his "Progress of the Working Classes", estimates that the capitalist classes receive from capital—excluding "wages of superintendence" and salaries—some £400,000,000 a year. In 1881, the income-tax returns quoted by Mr. Giffen show that the income from capital was no less than £407,000,000, and in estimating those in Schedules B and D (Part I.) Mr. Giffen certainly takes care to make the gains on "idle capital" as small as he can. Mr. Giffen takes the aggregate income of the whole nation at about £1,200,000,000, so that according to his own figures Capital takes more than a third part of the national income. I should be prepared to contend that the burden on the producers is heavier than he makes out, but even taking his own calculations the result is bad enough. For all this money which goes to capitalists is money *not* earned by the receivers—mark that all which is in any sense earned, as wages of superintendence, etc., is excluded—and by all this is lessened the share of the produce of labor which goes to labor.

We have already dealt with the way in which the worker suffers injustice when capital is invested in machinery owned by private individuals; we have now to consider the portion of it used as loans, cases in which the capitalist takes no part in the management of any industrial concern, but merely lends his money at usury, living on the interest he receives. There is so much confusion of thought on this subject, so much idea that a man has "a right" to invest money at interest, that it is necessary to try to get at the "bed-rock" of the question. Take the case of a man who earns 30s. in a week; suppose he spends 20s. and saves 10s. For the 20s. he spends he receives their equivalent in commodities, and these he consumes; he has had his "money's worth", and he is content, and if he requires more commodities he knows he must labor again to earn their equivalent in money. The 10s. he has saved, however, are to have a different fate; they represent, also, so much possibility of possession of their equivalent in commodities which he could consume; but he desires to defer this consumption to a future day, to defer it, perhaps, until he is too old to give labor in exchange for his needs. One might suppose that the equivalent of commodities for the 10s. would be as satisfactory as the equivalent of commodities for the 20s. But it is not so. He desires to invest his 10s. at interest; let us suppose he invests it at 5 per cent.; at the end of twenty years he will have received back his 10s. by instalments of 6d. a year, and will have exchanged it for 10s. worth of commodities; yet at the end of the twenty years he expects to receive back in addition his full 10s.; to have spent it all, and yet to find it undiminished; so that for his 10s. saved he expects to receive 20s. worth of commodities in twenty years, to have his labor paid for twice over. In the case of money only is it possible to eat your cake and have it, and after you have eaten it to pass it on as large as ever to your descendants, so that they may eat it and yet find it, like the widow's cruse, ever miraculously renewed.

Those who defend usury do so generally on its supposed collateral advantages, rather than on its central theory. It is argued that "*if a man gets no interest on his savings, he has no incitement to work*". To this it may be answered: (*a*) That there is clearly no incitement to work on the part of those who live on interest, since their money comes tumbling in whether they work or idle; it is the labor of others on which the interest-receiver lives. (*b*) That the incitement to work would be greater if the reward of work were not diminished by the imposition on it of a tax for the benefit of the idle; surely the abstraction of £400,000,000 annually for interest can hardly act as an incitement to those whose labor returns are diminished to that extent. (*c*) That the real incitement to work is the desire to possess the result of labor, and that the more completely that desire is satisfied the greater will the incitement become. Would the incitement to tramcar employees be lessened, if the necessity of paying 10 per cent. on shareholders' capital no longer kept down their wages? But, in truth, this argument as to incitement to workers is either ignorant, or disingenuous. The mainspring of the worker's toil is, as a matter of fact, compulsion, not the incitement of hope of reward. Had he control over the product of his own labor, then the desire to obtain more might incite him to work harder, as, indeed, has been found to be the case with piece-work, and in co-operative undertakings: with his fixed wage it is to him a matter of indifference how much or how little he produces. The desire for interest is an incitement to the capitalist to press his wage-toilers to work harder, so that after he has satisfied his own power of consumption he may lay by all the surplus value he can squeeze out of them, and increase the capital he has out at interest. The higher the interest obtainable, the greater the compulsion to work put upon the producers. But this compulsion is clearly an evil, not a good, and in the case of the tramcar employees just cited, it is compulsion which forces them to accept the long hours of labor, and the compulsion is exercised in order to obtain interest for the shareholders.

"*The incitement to thrift will disappear.*" But (*a*) the interest obtainable by "thrift" is too small to serve as an incitement, for the savings of the industrious poor are not sufficient to give interest enough to subsist on. The Savings Banks are resorted to as a convenient place wherein to put money saved for future use; it is the safe keeping of the money "for a rainy day", not the trifling interest, which is the attraction to the anxious poor. The small amount permitted to an individual and the low interest are sufficient proofs of this assertion; no one must put in more than £30 in a year, the interest is only 2½ per cent., and this is not paid yearly, but is added to the principal. And this future necessity is the real incitement to thrift. A man earns, say, sufficient this week to support himself for a fortnight; having satisfied his needs, he does not want to satisfy them twice over; he knows that some years hence his power of work will have disappeared, while his necessity of consumption will remain, and he defers his consumption of half the results of his labor till that time. Why should he look for added power of consumption as a reward for deferring his consumption for his own convenience? Without interest, thoughtful people would save, for the sake of comfort in their old age. It may however be conceded that the incitement to annex the results of the thrift of others—the only way in which big fortunes can be made—will disappear with the disappearance of interest, and the possibility of living idly by taxing the labor of others.

"*It will not be possible to get money for railroads, tramcars, etc., if interest on share capital disappears.*" But the indestructible reason for making railroads, tramways, etc., is the need for the conveniences they afford. And Socialism would place the making and carrying on of all means of transit in the hands of local bodies, municipalities, and so forth, who would raise the requisite funds from the community which is to enjoy the increased facilities. These funds would be used in remuneration of the labor expended on them, and none would have a right to levy a perpetual tax on the public on the pretence of having lent the money originally employed in the construction. Now a man claims the right to tax all future labors and all future consumers for the benefit of his posterity, as a reward for having worked and saved, or mostly as a reward for having transferred into his own pockets the results of his neighbor's toil. It is time that the immorality of this claim should be pointed out, and that people should be told that while they may rightly save and live on their savings, they ought not to use their savings for the enslavement and the taxing of other people. An effective step towards the abolition of interest might be taken by the closing of the sources of idle investment, the taking over by local bodies of the local means of transit, the gas and water supply, etc., while the central authority takes over the railways. The question of compensation would be solved with the least amount of injustice to exploiters and exploited by paying over a yearly dividend to shareholders until the dividends amounted to a sum equal to the nominal value of the shares held; thus a £100 share would be extinguished by the payment of a sum of £10 annually for ten years, leaving the shareholder richer than he was originally by all the interest received during the past, but terminating his right to tax within a brief period.

There is, however, one argument in favor of interest which brings conviction to many minds; an individual wants to perform a piece of productive work, but has no capital and is unable to do it; he borrows the capital and performs the work; since the man who lent the capital has facilitated the doing of the work, ought he not to share in the product, which would have had no existence but for his capital? Now it might be answered to this that if his capital is returned to him in full he has lost nothing by the transaction, but has, on the contrary, gained the advantage of having his money taken care of without trouble to himself, and returned to him uninjured at the time that he requires it. But the real answer is that interest is inevitable so long as Capital remains in private hands, so long as individuals are permitted to annex the results of the unpaid labor of others, and so manufacture a lien on all future industry. Interest will only be abolished when the results of the past unpaid labor of many are held by the many to facilitate the future labor of many. Now, industry can only be carried on with the permission and the assistance of those whose stores of wealth have been piled up for them by thousands of patient toilers; and that permission and assistance can only be gained by taxing labor for the enrichment of the lender. In the future those vast stores will be used to carry on production, and while labor will constantly replace the capital it uses in production, it will not also be taxed for the benefit of individuals. Interest and private property in the means of production must stand and fall together. At the present time no law against usury could be passed, and even were the passing of such a law possible it would be a dead letter, so thoroughly is the present system built on the paying of interest. All Socialists can do for the moment is to expose the fundamental dishonesty and injustice of usury, and so pave the way for a better state of things.

Apart from the abuse of Capital here indicated Capital has a function which, of course, no Socialist ignores. Capital is necessary for all forms of industry, and its function is: to save labor, as by machinery; to facilitate it, by the introduction of improvements therein; to support it while it is employed in production, and until its products are exchanged. The true use of the savings of past labor is to lighten future labor, to fertilise production. But in order that it may be thus used, it must be in the hands of the community instead of in the hands of individuals. Being as it is, and must be, the result of unpaid labor, it should pass to the community to be used for the common good, instead of to individuals to enrich them to the common loss.

Land.

It is hardly necessary to argue, at this time of day, that Land, *i.e.*, natural agents, ought not to be the private property of individuals. No absolute property in land is indeed recognised by the laws of this realm, but the proposition that land ought not to be private property goes, of course, much further than this legal doctrine. It declares that the soil on which a nation lives ought to belong to the nation; that those who cultivate it, or who mine in it, and who for practical purposes must have for the time the exclusive usufruct of portions of it, should pay into the national exchequer a duly-assessed sum, thus rendering an equivalent for the privilege they enjoy, and making the whole community sharers in the benefits derived from natural agents.

The present system of permitting private ownership of land has led to three great and increasing evils; the establishment of an idle class, which grows richer by increasingly taxing the industrious; the divorce of the really agricultural class from the soil; the exodus from the country districts into the towns.

Private ownership of natural agents must inevitably result in the first of these three evils. These natural agents are the basis of wealth; the very subsistence of the nation depends on their utilisation; yet a comparatively small class is permitted to claim them as private property, and to appropriate the rent to its private use. Hence, one of the first charges on the results of labor is rent, and rent, be it noted, not to the community, but to an individual who has acquired the legal right to stand between labor and land. Now just as wage is determined practically by the standard of living, so is rent determined by the same thing. The landlord exacts as rent the value of the produce minus the subsistence of the tenant, and in many cases, if the farmer's receipts sink and there is no corresponding lowering of rent, the farmer cannot even subsist, and becomes bankrupt. Hence, if a farmer improves the land and so obtains from it larger returns, the landlord steps in and raises his rent, claiming ever as his, produce minus subsistence, and confiscating for his own advantage the results of the labor and invested capital of the farmer. Thus also with the spread of commercial prosperity comes a rise in the tax levied by the landlords; as towns grow larger the land around them becomes more valuable, and thus the Stanleys grow wealthy by the growth of Liverpool, and the Grosvenors and Russells by that of London: competition drives up rents, and landlords may live in Italy or Turkey, and become ever wealthier by the growth of English trade, and the toil of English laborers. Moffat points out ("Economy of Consumption," p. 142) that part of the retailer's profit, and possibly the larger part of it "is purely local, and which he could not carry away with him. It distinguishes the site of his business, and resolves itself into rent. If the retailer owns his own premises, he may be content with this part of his profits, and handing the business to another become a landlord. If they are owned by another, the owner, unless the retailer is able to find other suitable premises within a moderate distance, will be able to levy all the extra profit from him in the shape of rent. Hence the rapid rise of rents in the central localities of large towns." Socialists are accused of desiring to confiscate property but the regular and uncensured confiscation of the property of busy people by idlers, the bloodsucking of the landlord leeches, pass unnoticed year by year, and Society honors the confiscators. The expropriation of small cultivators has been going on for the last 400 years, partly by big landlords buying up small ones, and partly by their thefts of common land. The story of Naboth's vineyard has been repeated in hundreds of country districts. The exorbitant rents demanded by landlords, with the pressure of American competition aided by capitalists on this side, have ruined the farming class, while the absorption of small holdings has turned into day-laborers at miserable wage the class that formerly were independent tillers of the soil. Attracted by the higher wage ruling in manufacturing towns this dislanded class has flocked into them, has crowded into unsuitable houses, increased the slums of our great cities, and, under most unwholesome conditions has multiplied with terrible rapidity. This exodus has been further quickened by the letting of formerly arable land for sheep-pasture, and the consequent forced migration of the no longer needed tillers. And thus have come about the under-population of the agricultural districts, and the over-crowding of cities: too few engaged in agricultural, and too many competing for industrial, employment; until we find our own land undercultivated, and even in some districts going out of cultivation, while food is being imported to an alarming extent, and the unemployed are becoming a menace to public tranquillity. The effect on England of revolution abroad is apt to be overlooked in studying our own labor difficulties. A considerable portion of our imports represents rent and interest from estates abroad and foreign investments. This portion would suddenly stop as regards any country in which a revolution occurred, and foreign workmen were, in consequence, no longer subjected to exploitation for the benefit of English capitalists. Now this likelihood of foreign revolution is yearly increasing, and Europe is becoming more and more like a boiler with armed forces sitting on the safety valve.

The first attempt to move in the right direction is the Land Cultivation Bill introduced into the House of Commons by Charles Bradlaugh. This proposes to expropriate landlords who hold cultivable land waste; to give them, as compensation, payment for twenty-five years equal in amount to the annual value of the produce obtained from the confiscated land—so that if there is no produce there will be no payment; to vest the land in the State, and to let it, not sell it, to cultivators. Thus, if the Bill passed, a large area of land would be nationalised early in next year. Such an Act, followed up by others taking over all land let on building leases as they run out—probably paying to the present landlords, for life, the original ground-rents; making the Land Tax an adequate rent paid to the State; taking back without compensation all common lands that have been stolen; breaking up the big estates by crushing taxation; steps like these, if taken with sufficient rapidity, may effect a complete Land Revolution without violence, and establish Socialism so far as the ownership of natural agents is concerned.

It is of vital importance to progress in a Socialist direction that an uncompromising resistance should be offered to all schemes for the creation of new proprietors of the soil. Peasant cultivators, paying rent to the State, are good. Peasant proprietors are a mere bulwark, raised by landlords to guard their own big estates, and will delay the realisation of the true theory that the State should be the only landowner. It is also important that Socialists should popularise the idea of communal, or co-operative, farming. There can be no doubt that cereal crops can be raised most economically on large holdings, and such holdings should be rented from the body or bodies representing the community by groups of cultivators, so that both large and small farms should be found in agricultural districts. But it must be distinctly stated that the Socialisation of Land without the Socialisation of Capital will not solve the social problem. No replanting of the people in the soil, no improved balance of agricultural and industrial production, will by themselves free the wage-slaves of our towns. Means of production, as well as natural agents, must come under the control of the community, before the triumph of Socialism can be complete. The tendency of Radicals to aim only at the nationalisation of land has an effect, however, which will ultimately prove of service. It irritates the landlord class, and the landlords devote themselves to proving that there is no essential difference between property in Land and property in Capital. Just as they helped to pass the Factory Acts to restrain capitalists as a retort for the capitalist agitation against the Corn Laws, so they will be likely to help in nationalising Capital in revenge for the nationalisation of Land.

Education.

For the successful maintenance of a Socialist State a wide and thorough system of national education is an absolute necessity. A governed people may afford to be ignorant; a self-ruling community must be instructed, or it must perish. And the education contemplated by Socialism is a very different thing from the paltry modicum of knowledge deemed sufficient for the "masses" to-day. Under our present system education is a matter of class, and it is a misnomer to call it "national"; it is partly supported by the parents of the children who attend the Board

Schools, and partly by the rates and taxes; it is limited to the mere elements of learning; the one object of the teachers is to cram the children so that they may pass stated examinations, and thus obtain a Government grant per head. Under Socialism the whole system will be revolutionised, as the one aim then will be to educate in such a way as will ensure the greatest possible healthy development of the young, with a view to their future position as members of a free community.

The foundations of complete social equality will be laid in the school. All the children will be educated in the communal schools, the only distinction being that of age. Boys and girls will not be separated as they are now, but a common education will prepare for common work. Every child will be led through a course, which will embrace a thorough training in the elements of the various sciences, so that in after life he may feel an intelligent interest in each, and if his taste so lead him acquire later a fuller knowledge of any special branches. He—and "he" here includes "she"—will be instructed also in the elements of art, so that the sense of beauty may be developed and educated, and the refining influence of instructed taste may enrich both mind and manners. A knowledge of history, of literature, and of languages will widen sympathy and destroy narrowness and national prejudices. Nor will physical training be forgotten; gymnastics, dancing, riding, athletic games, will educate the senses and the limbs, and give vigor, quickness, dexterity, and robustness to the frame. To this will be superadded technical training, for these educated, cultured, graceful lads and lasses are to be workers, every one of them. The foundations of this technical training will be the same for all; all will learn to cook and scrub, to dig and sew, and to render quick assistance in accidents; it is probable also that the light portions of household duties will form part of the training of every child. But as the child grows into the youth, natural capacities will suggest the special training which should be given, so as to secure for the community the full advantages which might accrue from the varied abilities of its members. No genius then will be dwarfed by early neglect, no rare ability then perish for lack of culture. Individuality will then at last find full expression, and none will need to trample on his brother in order to secure full scope for his own development. It is probable that each will learn more than a single trade—an easy task when brain acuteness and manual dexterity have been cultured—so as to promote adaptability in the future industrial life.

Now to many, I fear to most, of my readers, this sketch of what education will be in a Socialist community will appear a mere Utopian dream. Yet is it not worth while for such to ask themselves: Why should not such an education be the natural lot of every child in a well-ordered community? Is there anything in it superfluous for the thorough development of the faculties of a human being? And if it be admitted that boys and girls thus educated would form nobler, completer, more many-sided human beings than are the men and women of to-day, is it not a rational thing to set up as an object to be worked for the realisation of an idea which would prove of incalculable benefit to the community?

It is hardly necessary to add that education, in a Socialist State, would be "free"—*i.e.*, supported at the public cost, and compulsory. Free, because the education of the young is of vital importance to the community; because class distinctions can only be effaced by the training of children in common schools; because education is too important a matter to be left to the whims of individuals, and if it be removed from the parent's direction and supervision it is not just to compel him to pay for it. Compulsory, because the State cannot afford to leave its future citizens ignorant and helpless, and it is bound to protect its weak members against injustice and neglect.

Two objections are likely to be raised: the question of cost, and the question of unfitting persons for "the dirty work of the world, which someone must do".

As to cost. It must not be forgotten that this education is proposed for a Socialist community. In such a State there would be no idle adult class to be supported, but all would be workers, so that the wealth produced would be much greater than at the present time. Now according to the figures of anti-Socialist Mr. Giffen, the aggregate income of the people is at present about £1,200,000,000; of this the workers are assigned by him £620,000,000; deduct another £100,000,000 for return from investments abroad; this leaves £480,000,000 absorbed by the nonproducing class. (It must be remembered, further, that a large number of the "workers" are unnecessary distributors, whose powers could be utilised to much better purpose than is done to-day.) The wealth producers have to bear the Church on their shoulders, and provide it with an income variously stated at from £6,000,000 to £10,000,000 a year. They have to bear the "landed interest", with its appropriation in rents, royalties, etc., of something like £200,000,000. They have to bear the ultimate weight of imperial and local taxation, estimated at about £120,000,000 for the present year. All these charges, by whomsoever nominally paid, have to come out of the wealth produced by the workers. Is it then to be pretended that when the idle class has disappeared there will not be wealth enough produced for the education of the children, or that their education will be as heavy a burden as the drones are to-day? Nor must it be forgotten that there are millions of acres of land that would produce wealth if labor were sent to them, and that plenty of our idlers will there find productive work which will enormously increase the national wealth. Nor also that the waste which results from luxurious idle living will be of the past, and that a simpler, manlier rate of expenditure will have replaced the gluttony and intemperance now prevalent in the "higher circles of society".

But it will indeed be of vital importance that the proportion of workers to non-workers shall be considered, and that there shall not be in a Socialist community the overlarge families which are a characteristic of the present system. Families of ten or a dozen children belong to the capitalist system, which requires for its success a numerous and struggling proletariat, propagating with extreme rapidity, so as to keep up a plentiful supply of men, women, and children for the labor-market, as well as a supply of men for the army to be food for cannon, and women for the streets to be food for lust. Under a Socialist régime, the community will have something to say as to the numbers of the new members that are to be introduced into it, and for many years supported by it; and it will prefer a reasonable number of healthy, well-educated children, to a yearly huge increase which would overburden its industry.

As to unfitting persons for work. So long as manual work is regarded as degrading, education, by increasing sensitiveness to public opinion, tends to make people shrink from it, at least if their sensitiveness is greater than their intelligence. But even now an educated person of strong will and clear judgment, who knows that all useful work is worthy of respect, finds that his education fits him to perform work more quickly and more intelligently than is possible to an ignorant person; and respecting himself in its thorough accomplishment he is conscious of no degradation. Weak persons, compelled to labor for their bread, and aware that manual work is considered to place the worker in a subordinate social class, feel ashamed of the inferior position assigned to them by public opinion; and knowing by experience that they will be snubbed if they treat their "superiors" as equals, they live down to their social rank, and long to raise their children into a class above their own. One consequence of the absurd artificial disadvantage attached to manual work, is that the children of the more successful workers crowd the inferior professional occupations, and a man prefers to be a clerk or a curate on £90 a year to being an artisan on £150. But in the Socialist State only idleness will be despised, and all useful work will be honored. There is nothing more intrinsically degrading in driving a plough than in driving a pen, although the ploughman is now relegated to the kitchen while the clerk is received in the drawing-room. The distinction is primarily a purely artificial one, but it is made real by educating the one type while the other is left ignorant, and by teaching the one to look on his work as work "fit for a gentleman", while the other is taught that his work is held in low social esteem. Each reflects the surrounding public opinion, and accepts the position assigned by it. In Socialism, both will be educated together as children; both will be taught to look on all work as equally honorable, if useful to the community; both will be cultured "gentlemen", following each his natural bent; the ploughman will be as used to his pen as the clerk; the clerk as ready to do heavy work as the ploughman; and as public opinion will regard them as equals and will hold them in equal honor, neither will feel any sense of superiority or inferiority, but they will meet on common ground as men, as members of a social unity. As to the physically unpleasant work—such as dealing with sewers, dung-heaps, etc.—much of that will probably be done by machinery, when there is no helpless class on whose shoulders it may be bound. Such as cannot be done by machinery, will probably be divided among a large number, each taking a small share thereof, and the amount done by each will thus become so insignificant, that it will be but slightly felt. In any case the profound selfishness, which would put all burden on a helot class, and rather see it brutalised by the crushing weight than bear a portion of the load on one of its fingers, must be taught that Socialism means equality, and that the divine right of idlers, to live at ease on the labor of others and to be shielded by the bodies of the poor from all the unpleasantnesses of the world, is one of the notions against which Socialism wars, and which must follow the correlative superstition of the divine right of kings.

JUSTICE.

The pretence that under the present system there is one law for rich and poor is so barefaced a piece of impudence, that it is hardly worth while to refute it. Everyone knows that a rich man is fined for an offence for which a poor man is sent to gaol; that no wise man goes to law unless he has plenty of money; that in a litigation between a rich and a poor man, the poor man practically stands no chance, for even if he at first succeeds the rich man can appeal, and secure in the power of his money-bags wear out his poor antagonist by costly delays and by going from court to court. The poor man cannot fee first-class counsel, seek out and bring up his witnesses from various parts of the country, and keep a stream of money continually running through his solicitor's hands. There might be the same law for him as for the rich man, if he could get it; but it is far away behind a golden gate, and he lacks the key which alone will fit the wards of the lock. Yet surely one of the primary duties of a State is to do justice among its members, and to prevent the oppression of the weak by the strong. In a civilised State justice should be dealt out without fee or reward; if a man gives up his inherent right to defend himself and to judge in his own quarrel, he ought not to be placed in a worse position than he would be in if society did not exist. Lawyers, like judges, should be officials paid by the State, and should have no pecuniary interest in winning the case in which they are engaged.

The administration of justice in a Socialist State will be a very much simpler matter than it is now. Most crimes arise from the desire to become rich, from poverty, and from ignorance. Under Socialism poverty and ignorance will have disappeared, and the desire to grow rich will have no *raison d'être* when everyone has sufficient for comfort, is free from anxiety as to his future, and sees above him no wealthy idlers whose luxury he desires to ape, and whose idleness is held up to him as a matter of envy, as the ideal state for man.

AMUSEMENT.

There is a curious inconsistency in the way in which people deal with the question of amusement at the present time. We should have an outcry about "pauperisation" and "interference with private enterprise", if anyone proposed that the theatres should be open to the public without charge. Yet Hyde Park is kept gorgeous with flowers, Rotten Row is carefully attended to, a whole staff of workers is employed, in order that the wealthy may have a fashionable and pleasant lounge; and all this is done at the national expense, without any expression of fear lest the wealthy should be pauperised by this expenditure on their behalf. Nor is complaint made of the public money spent on the other parks in London; the most that is suggested is that the money wanted ought to be taken from the London rates and not from the national taxes. No one proposes that the parks should be sold to the highest bidder, and that private enterprise should be encouraged by permitting some capitalist to buy them, and to make a charge at the gate for admission. It is significant that once anything gets under State control, the advantages are found to be so great that no one would dream of bringing it back under private exploitation. In some parks a band plays, and people are actually demoralised by listening to music for which they do not pay directly. Nay more; the British Museum, the National Gallery, the South Kensington Museum, are all open free, and no one's dignity is injured. But if the National Gallery be open free, why not the Royal Academy? If a band may be listened to in the open air without payment, why not in a concert room? And if a concert may be free, why not a theatre? Under the present system, the Royal Academy, the concert, the theatre, are all private speculations, and the public is exploited for the profit of the speculators. The National Gallery and the Museums are national property, and the nation enjoys the use of its own possessions. In a nation which has gone so far in the direction of providing intellectual amusement, it cannot be pretended that any principle is involved in the question whether or not it shall go further along the same road. A nation which collects the works of dead painters can hardly, on principle, refuse to show the works of living ones; and we Socialists may fairly urge the success of what has already been done in the way of catering for the public amusement as a reason for doing more.

As it is, with the exception of a few places, the poor, whose lives most need the light of amusement and of beauty, are relegated to the very lowest and coarsest forms of recreation. Unreal and intensely vulgar pictures of life are offered them at the theatres which specially cater for them; they never have the delight of seeing really graceful dancing, or noble acting, or of hearing exquisite music. Verily, the amusements of the wealthier leave much to be desired, and theatre and music-hall alike pander to a low and vulgar taste instead of educating and refining it; but still these are better than their analogues at the East End. Under Socialism, the theatre will become a great teacher instead of a catch-penny spectacle; and dramatists and actors alike will work for the honor of a noble art, instead of degrading their talents to catch the applause of the most numerous class of an uneducated people. Then an educated public will demand a higher art, and artists will find it worth while to study when patient endeavor meets with public recognition, and crude impertinence suffers its due reproof. Theatres, concerts, parks, all places of public resort, will be communal property, open alike to all, and controlled by elected officers.

Conclusion.

It remains, in conclusion, to note the chief objections raised to Socialism by its opponents. Of these the most generally urged are three: that it will check individual initiative and energy; that it will destroy individuality; that it will unduly restrict personal liberty.

That it will check individual initiative and energy. This objection is founded on the idea that the impulse to initiative must always be desire for personal money gain. But this idea flies directly in the face of facts. Even under the individualistic system, no great discovery has ever been made and proclaimed merely from desire for personal money profit. The genius that invents is moved by an imperial necessity of its own nature, and wealth usually falls to the lot of the commonplace man who exploits the genius, and not to the genius itself. Even talent is moved more by joy in its own exercise, and in the public approval it wins, than by mere hope of money gain. Who would not rather be an Isaac Newton, a Shelley, or a Shakspere, than a mere Vanderbilt? And most of all are those of strong individual initiative moved by desire to serve their "larger self", which is Man. The majority of such choose the unpopular path, and by sheer strength and service gradually win over the majority. We see men and women who might have won wealth, position, power, by using their talents for personal gain in pursuits deemed honorable, cheerfully throw all aside to proclaim an unpopular truth, and to serve a cause they believe to be good and useful. And these motives will become far more powerful under Socialism than they are now. For the possession of money looms unduly large to-day in consequence of the horrible results of the want of it. The dread of hunger and of charity is the microscope which magnifies the value of wealth. But once let all men be secure of the necessaries and comforts of life, and all the finer motives of action will take their proper place. Energy will have its full scope under Socialism, and indeed when the value of a man's work is secured to him instead of the half being appropriated by someone else, it will receive a new impulse. How great will be the incentive to exertion when the discovery of some new force, or new application of a known force, means greater comfort for the discoverer *and* for all; none thrown out of work by it, none injured by it, but so much solid gain for each. And for the discoverer, as well as the material gain common to him and his comrades, the thanks and praise of the community in which he lives. And let not the power of public opinion be undervalued as a stimulus to exertion. What Greek athlete would have sold his wreath of bay for its weight in gold? Only one kind of energy will be annihilated by Socialism—the energy that enslaves others for its own gain, and exploits its weaker brethren for its own profit. For this kind of energy there will be no room. The coarse purse-proud mediocrity, who by sheer force of pushing brutality has trampled his way to the front, will have vanished. The man who grows rich by underpaying his employees, by being a "hard business man", will have passed away. Energy will have to find for itself paths of service instead of paths of oppression, and will be honored or reprobated according to the way in which it is used.

That it will destroy individuality. If this were true, the loss to progress would indeed be incalculable. But Socialism, instead of destroying individuality will cultivate and accentuate it, and indeed will make it possible for the first time in civilisation for the vast majority. For it needs, in order that individuality shall be developed, that the individual shall have his characteristics drawn out and trained by education; it needs that he shall work, in maturity, at the work for which his natural abilities fit him; it needs that he shall not be exhausted by excessive toil, but shall go fresh and vigorous to his labor; it needs that he shall have leisure to continuously improve himself, to train his intellect and his taste. But such education, such choice of work, such short hours of labor, such leisure for self-culture, where are all these to-day for our laboring population? A tremendous individuality, joined to robust health, may make its way upward out of the ranks of the handworkers to-day; but all normal individuality is crushed out between the grinding-stones of the industrial mill. See the faces of the lads and lasses as they troop out of the factory, out of the great mercantile establishments; how alike they all are! They might almost have been turned out by the dozen. We Socialists demand that individuality shall be possible for all, and not only for the few who are too strong to crush.

That it will unduly restrict personal liberty. Socialism, as conceived by the non-student of it, is an iron system, in which the "State"—which is apparently separate from the citizens—shall rigidly assign to each his task, and deal out to each his subsistence. Even if this caricature were accurate, Socialism would give the great majority far more freedom than they enjoy to-day; for they would only be under the yoke for their brief hours of toil, and would have unfettered freedom for the greater portion of their time. Contrast this compulsion with the compulsion exercised on the workers to-day by the sweater, the manager of the works or business, and above all the compulsion of hunger, that makes them bend to the yoke for the long hours of the working day, and often far into the night: and then say whether the "freedom" of Industrialism is not a heavier chain than the "tyranny" of the most bureaucratic Socialism imagined by our opponents. But the "tyranny of Socialism", however, would consist only in ordering—and enforcing the order if necessary—that every healthy adult should labor for his own subsistence. That is, it would protect the liberty of each by not allowing anyone to compel another person to work for him, and by opening to all equal opportunities of working for themselves. The worker would choose his own work certainly as freely as he does now: at the present time, if one class of work has enough operatives employed at it, a man must take some other, and I do not see that Socialism could prevent this limitation of choice. At any rate, the limitation is not an argument against Socialism, since it exists at the present time.

Imagine the glorious freedom which would be the lot of each when, the task of social work complete, and done under healthy and pleasant conditions, the worker turned to science, literature, art, gymnastics, to what he would, for the joyous hours of leisure. For him all the treasures of knowledge and of beauty; for him all the delights of scenery and of art; for him all that only the wealthy enjoy to-day; all that comes from work flowing back to enrich the worker's life.

I know that our hope is said to be the dream of the enthusiast; I know that our message is derided, and that the gospel of man's redemption which we preach is scorned. Be it so. Our work shall answer the gibes of our opponents, and our faith in the future shall outlast their mockery. We know that however much man's ignorance may hinder our advance; however much his selfishness may block our path; that we shall yet win our way to the land we have seen but in our visions, and rear the temple of human happiness on the solid foundation stones of science and of truth. Above all sneer and taunt, above all laughter and bitter cries of hatred, rings out steadily our prophecy of the coming time:

"O nations undivided,
O single People, and free,
We dreamers, we derided,
We mad blind men that see,
We bear you witness ere ye come that ye shall be."